The History of JUNGLE GARDENS

The History of

JUNGLE
GARDENS

THE HISTORY OF JUNGLE GARDENS
Lisa B. Osborn
Shane K. Bernard
Scott Carroll

Copyright © 2010 by Jungle Gardens, Inc.
All Rights Reserved
Printed in the United States of America
First Edition — April 2010

Library of Congress Control Number: 2009937064

ISBN: 978-0-615-32211-7

Book and cover design: Scott Carroll, Scott Carroll Designs, Inc.
www.scottcarrolldesigns.com

Unless stated otherwise, all text and images in this book are property of or have been licensed by Jungle Gardens, Inc., and may not be reproduced without explicit permission. Jungle Gardens, Inc., has made every effort to properly credit ownership and/or determine ownership of each image.

The image of Pauline "Polly" McIlhenny Simmons and Edward McIlhenny Simmons on page 111 appears courtesy of the New Orleans *Times-Picayune*.

The image of the Ethyl Corporation advertisement on page 79 appears courtesy of the Ethyl Corporation/NewMarket Corporation, Richmond, Virginia.

The following images appear courtesy of the I. A. and Carroll Martin Photo Collection, Iberia Parish Library, New Iberia, Louisiana: entrance arch (Image #10900M), page 14; Tabasco sauce factory (#0308), page 27; egret nesting rack at upper left corner (#01901F), page 64; black-and-white alligator photographs (#10901B, #10901C, #10901D, #10901E), pages 70-71; wisteria tunnel (#10941), page 96.

TABASCO® is a registered trademark for sauces and other goods and services; TABASCO, the TABASCO bottle design and label designs are the exclusive property of McIlhenny Company, Avery Island, LA 70513 USA.

"Little Gidding" (excerpt) by T. S. Eliot, from *Four Quartets* copyright 1943 and renewed 1971 by Esme Valerie Eliot.

All recent photography of Jungle Gardens © 2010 Dean Cavalier.

www.JUNGLEGARDENS.org

Jungle Gardens, Inc.
P.O. Box 126
Avery Island LA 70513

"MY GARDEN"

MY GARDEN IS A LOVELY PLACE
WHERE IRISES AND LILIES RACE,
TO MATCH AZALEAS' BRILLIANT HUES
WITH ORANGE, YELLOW, REDS AND BLUES

MY GARDEN IS A PLACE I LOVE
WHERE MOCKING BIRD AND COOING DOVE
THEIR JOYOUS VOICES RAISE EACH DAY
KNOWING NO HARM WILL COME THEIR WAY

MY GARDEN IS A PLACE WHERE BEST
ALL WOE AND PAIN IS LAID AT REST
AND HAPPY PLANTS FROM EAST AND WEST
THEIR LIFE THEY DRAW FROM EARTH'S WARM
BREAST.

FLOWERS AND BIRDS ARE ON DISPLAY
MAKING MY GARDEN BRIGHT AND GAY
AND WHEN I WALK WHERE THE BLOSSOMS NOD
I FEEL MY GARDEN IS CLOSE TO GOD!

ACKNOWLEDGEMENTS

The authors wish to thank Harold G. Osborn III for his guidance on this project, Dorothy Ball for editing the manuscript, and Jungle Gardens, Inc. — particularly its president, Edward McIlhenny Simmons — for underwriting this publication.

We also extend our thanks to Donna Neuville, Lisa F. Grant, and Cindy Fremin for their assistance with the project's administration.

Finally, we offer our sincerest thanks to two people whose assistance proved invaluable throughout the book's creation — Dean Cavalier, for his design suggestions and photography of present-day Jungle Gardens, and Shannon Glock, for her finishing touches to the graphic layout.

In tribute to
EDWARD AVERY McILHENNY
(1872-1949)

We shall not cease from exploration

And the end of all our exploring

Will be to arrive where we started

And know the place for the first time.

— T. S. Eliot, "Little Gidding"

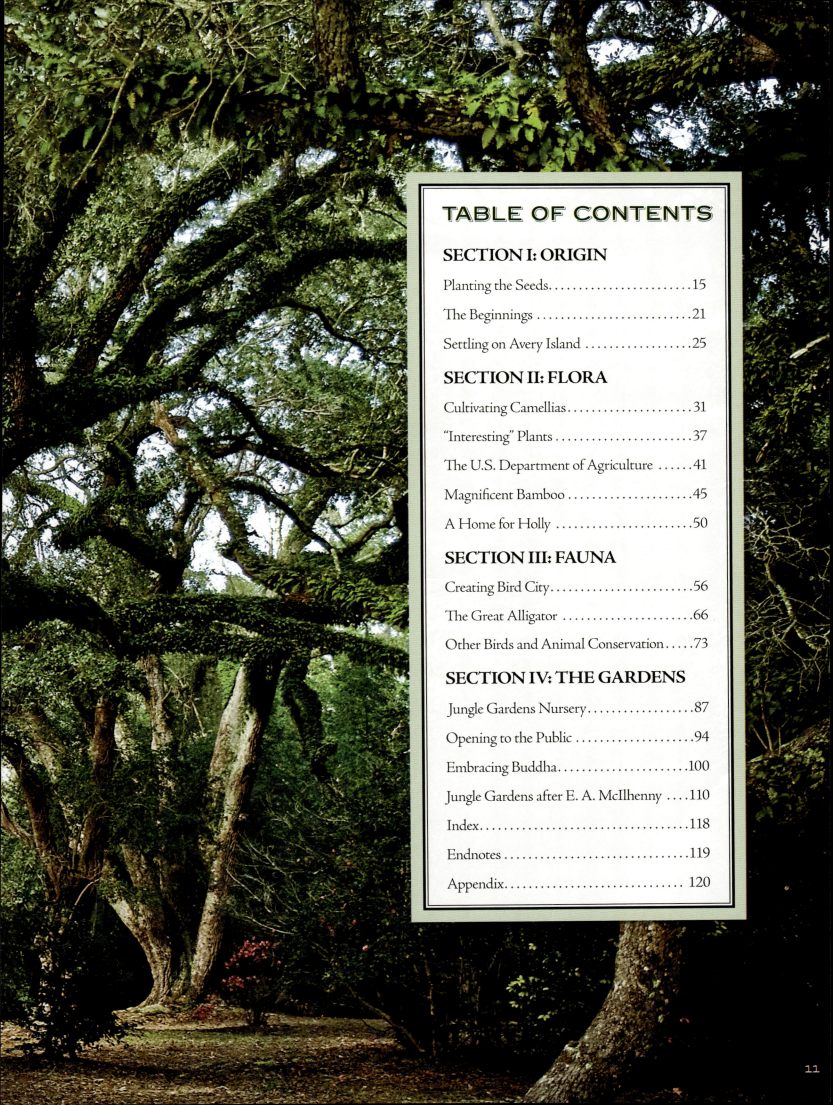

TABLE OF CONTENTS

SECTION I: ORIGIN
Planting the Seeds........................15

The Beginnings 21

Settling on Avery Island 25

SECTION II: FLORA
Cultivating Camellias.....................31

"Interesting" Plants 37

The U.S. Department of Agriculture 41

Magnificent Bamboo 45

A Home for Holly 50

SECTION III: FAUNA
Creating Bird City........................56

The Great Alligator 66

Other Birds and Animal Conservation.....73

SECTION IV: THE GARDENS
Jungle Gardens Nursery...................87

Opening to the Public 94

Embracing Buddha.......................100

Jungle Gardens after E. A. McIlhenny 110

Index...................................118

Endnotes 119

Appendix............................... 120

SECTION I:

The ORIGIN of JUNGLE GARDENS

Original entrance to Jungle Gardens, circa 1940.

Planting THE SEEDS

On the northwest side of Avery Island, along Bayou Petite Anse, lie 170 acres of gentle rolling landscape known as *Jungle Gardens*. Sweeping lawns are sheltered by majestic live oaks. Groves of countless camellias bloom from October to March, azaleas of surprising color float like mist around the trees, and bamboos from Asia range in color from yellow to sky blue. The gardens sport both exotic and native plants, some of which explode into colorful blossoms or berries, or just add to the rich texture of the greenery. Alligators live in Jungle Gardens along with deer, turtles, bears and the many inhabitants of the Bird City wildfowl refuge. A centuries-old Buddha sits in a temple overlooking its own reflecting pool and garden.

Jungle Gardens occupies 170 acres on the northwest side of Avery Island.

It is a curious, mysterious, beautiful landscape. Visitors come to enjoy Jungle Gardens, sometimes as a pleasant park or, often, as a birding and wild animal refuge — yet few visitors know how the gardens came to be or understand the extraordinary ideas behind its creation. This is the story of how Jungle Gardens began, as well as the role it played in the conservation movement and in the introduction of new plant species to the United States. It also is an exploration of the Gardens' sublime nature and of the insight and energy that shaped it.

Many of the photographs in this book were taken by the dynamic architect of Jungle Gardens, E. A. McIlhenny. The pictures chronicle his consuming fascination with and reverence for the natural world. He began the gardens as an extension of his home grounds, enhancing his bird sanctuary with rare and unusual plants. Eventually, the grounds served as a kind of Ellis Island for many foreign, particularly Asian, plants as yet unknown in America. Some, like holly and bamboo, found Jungle Gardens an especially fertile home. Here, too, the more local, decrepit beauties of the fashionable pre-Civil War camellias were propagated and restored to exquisite loveliness.

Jungle Gardens was a glorious experiment in making the fertile land of south Louisiana produce for, thrive under, and support her people and wildlife. This experiment gave rise decades later to Avery Island's motto, "Man and Environment in Balance," a theme that embraces a complex understanding of nature and the role of personal responsibility in conservation.

Above, Avery Island's "Man and Environment in Balance" logo, created by McIlhenny Company in 1971.

Top, McIlhenny in water garden, circa 1940.

Left, E. A. McIlhenny photographing in a pirogue, circa 1920.

McIlhenny's mother, Mary Eliza Avery McIlhenny, circa 1900.

The
BEGINNINGS

The seeds for Jungle Gardens were sown in the early 1880s, when young Edward Avery McIlhenny, second son of Tabasco sauce inventor Edmund McIlhenny, often explored Avery Island with his siblings and cousins. Even as a child, McIlhenny expressed deep interest in the plants and animals of his fertile Louisiana home. While fishing with his uncles and cousins, he paid more attention to the behavior of large wading birds hunting along the bayous than in the excitement of a big fish being hauled in. He wondered about the birds' other activities, and spent much of his time observing and tracking wildfowl to discover their habits and routines.

Early on, family and tutors deemed McIlhenny an unusually capable child. They regarded him as an extremely good and careful shot, and permitted him to spend days at a time out in the marsh hunting, studying, and exploring. Even as a boy, he was keenly observant, and the time he spent in the natural world allowed him to develop an unusually profound understanding of birds, plants, animals, and the land. Furthermore, that understanding gave him an awareness of the delicate and interconnected relationships that bound them all together.

McIlhenny had a particularly complex understanding of the destruction that man could inflict on the natural world by disrupting its fragile balance. When skin and plume hunters came to the Louisiana marshes in the 1880s, McIlhenny saw how damage to the bird and alligator populations exerted an even broader effect, causing less obvious but equally dramatic injury to the marshes and the wild places around Avery Island. Since most of the bird slaughter stemmed from a demand for wispy feathers to embellish ladies' hats, McIlhenny took action, establishing a private wildfowl refuge in Jungle Gardens and addressing women consumers directly in an early conservation film titled *The Snowy Egret and Its Extermination* (1913).

Above, Edward Avery McIlhenny, circa 1877.

Above right, McIlhenny's daughters and Avery cousins, circa 1910.

Left, Edward Avery McIlhenny, circa 1876.

THE NIDOLOGIST

E. A. McILHENNY

Ornithologist and Oologist

AND

ECTOR OF NATURAL HISTORY SPECIMENS

Avery's Island, Iberia Parish, La.

*

K, OOLOGISTS!   LOOK AT THIS

PRICE LIST

Eggs in Fine Original Sets with Careful D

ST BE PAID BY PURCHASER ON ALL ORDERS UNDER FIVE DOLLARS

	per set		per set
@	$ 12	Fla. Nighthawk 8 sets of 2 eggs @	$
@	12	Baird's Woodpecker 4 sets of 6 eggs @	
	15	Golden-fronted Woodpecker, 10 sets of 4 eggs @	
eggs @	35	Central America Pileated Woodpecker, 2 of 5 @	
	75	Red-bellied Woodpecker, 3 sets of 5 eggs @	
	20	Mex. Crested Flycatcher, 10 sets of 4 eggs @	
	35	Crested Flycatcher, 20 sets of four eggs @	
	15	Kingbird, 50 sets of 4 eggs @	
ght Heron, 20 sets of 6 eggs @	20	Green Jay, 3 sets of 8 eggs @	
Egret, 10 sets of 4 eggs @	20	Brown Jay, 5 sets of 4 eggs @	
Egret, 25 sets of 4 eggs @	50	Lessons Oriole, 5 sets of 5 egg @	
per Rail, 5 sets of 10 eggs @	75	Orchard Oriole, 50 sets of 5 eggs @	
l, 3 sets of 10 eggs @	30	Great-tailed Grackle, 20 sets of 3 eggs @	
allinule, 5 sets of 9 eggs @	3 00	Boat-tailed Grackle, 50 sets of 3 eggs @	
10 sets of 4 eggs @	90	Fla. Grackle, 6 sets of 6 eggs @	
white, 2 sets of 12 eggs @	75	Dusky Seaside Sparrow, 5 sets of 4 eggs @	
obwhite, 5 sets of 11 eggs @	35	Texan Seaside Sparrow, 3 sets of 4 eggs @	
nged Dove, 10 sets of 2 eggs @	1 10	Cardinal, 20 sets of 3 eggs @	
and Dove, 10 sets of 2 eggs @	1 00	Gray-tailed Cardinal, 6 sets of 4 eggs @	
Dove, 10 sets of 2 egg @	15	Abert's Towhee, 10 sets of 3 eggs @	
Dove, 20 sets of 2 eggs @	25	Sennett's Thrasher, 10 sets of 4 eggs @	
ture, 20 sets of 2 egg @	30	Short-tailed Wren, 5 sets of 4 eggs @	
Vulture, 11 sets of 2 eggs @	05	Mockingbird, 20 sets of 4 eggs @	
Hawk, 10 sets of 3 eggs @	60	Bluebird, 20 sets of 4 eggs @	
led Hawk, 10 sets of 3 eggs @	60	Mexican Jacana, 10 sets of 5 eggs @	
Nighthawk, 10 sets of 2 eggs @	50	Chachalaca, 10 sets of 3 eggs @	
	25	Rose-throated Becard, 10 sets of 4 eggs @	

ve these eggs in fine series of sets, they are finely prepared, and have good scientific data.
d, and will be filled to your satisfaction. Here is a chance for Oologists to buy a lot of sets
such prices that there will be a profit in it for you.   This is the way to get a collection.   I am selli
ces only because I leave for Alaska in the spring and wish to close out before I go.

Settling on
AVERY ISLAND

McIlhenny decided on a career as a biologist and in 1894 at age twenty-two he served as ornithologist to explorer Frederick Cook on an ill-fated expedition to the Arctic. (The expedition ended when their ship, the *Miranda*, struck a reef and sank off the coast of Greenland.) Two years later, McIlhenny advertised his services in the *Nidologist*, a journal dedicated to the study of birds' nests, listing over 150 types of nests and eggs that "E. A. McIlhenny, Ornithologist and Oologist and General Collector of Natural History Specimens" could acquire for collectors. In 1897 at age twenty-five, he headed his own expedition to Point Barrow, Alaska, commissioned by two museums to collect Arctic biological and anthropological specimens.

While he was setting up his camp at Point Barrow, drift ice trapped and sank several nearby whaling ships, and McIlhenny found himself joined

Top left, McIlhenny photos from Point Barrow, Alaska, 1897-1898.
Middle left, Print advertisement for McIlhenny's services as a collector of biological specimens, 1897.
Above left, McIlhenny in arctic furs, circa 1897-1898.

by more than a hundred shipwrecked sailors.¹ He took charge, relieving the company of weapons, rationing his personal supplies (meant to last two years), hunting local game to feed the men, and providing them with rudimentary medical care. He managed to keep the rough company alive through the long winter, as well as to fulfill most of his obligations to the sponsoring museums.

In 1898, when he was twenty-six, McIlhenny's widowed mother asked him to take over the family's Tabasco pepper sauce business. So he returned to Avery Island, built his house on a hill overlooking Willow Pond, married, had children, and applied his curious skills to running a small, part-time family business, looking out for his mother and other extended family, and containing his boundless curiosity, abilities, and vigor to an isolated island.

Left, Mayward Hill, McIlhenny's home above Bird City.

Top, Tabasco sauce factory with cold frames (in foreground) for growing peppers, circa 1920.

Above, Advertisements for Tabasco sauce, circa 1900.

27

SECTION II:

The

FLORA

of

JUNGLE GARDENS

Previous spread, right,
Camellias, photographed
by McIlhenny.

Cultivating CAMELLIAS

Camellias were fabulously popular in mid-nineteenth-century Europe. Admired by celebrities and the aristocracy, many varieties were considered essential for chic gardens of the time. Naturally, the fashion spread to the gardens of Gallic and Francophile plantation owners in south Louisiana. As a result, antebellum planters imported camellias from France to enhance their gardens and their reputations. Although the Civil War put an end to extravagant gardening, many of the camellias continued to thrive on their own in the region's rich soil and semitropical climate.

While visiting old plantation gardens along Bayou Teche, young McIlhenny rediscovered the forgotten and now unfashionable camellias. Around 1900 he began to collect these surviving camellia shrubs and by 1902 he possessed over one hundred varieties in Jungle Gardens. Two of his better-known finds were Vedrine [sic] — discovered at a gas station in Vidrine, Louisiana, a small Evangeline Parish town to which many camellias were sent prior to the Civil War — and Governor Mouton, found and probably originally developed near Carencro, Louisiana, at the home of Louisiana Governor Alexandre Mouton (1804-1885).

Camellias and their horticulture intrigued McIlhenny, who combed catalogs and journals for information and for other varieties to enhance his collection. During the 1930s he imported hundreds of varieties from foreign nurseries, the most notable of which were T. J. Seidel in Dresden, Germany; Guichard Soeurs in Nantes, France; Chugai Shokubutsu in Kobe, Japan; K. Yashiroda, Ltd., in Kagaaken, Japan; and Robert Veitch & Sons, Ltd., in Exeter, England. Because of quarantine laws, imported plants could not be shipped with much protective dirt, so the mortality rate for these imports was high. Now an experienced gardener, McIlhenny succeeded in nursing back to health almost all the damaged plants he received. He was among the first gardeners in the United States to successfully grow *Camellia sasanqua* and *Camellia reticulata*. In addition to increasing his collection through the acquisition of local and imported plants, McIlhenny grew many thousands of camellias from seeds, as well as through grafting and root cutting. If after several years the resulting flower proved worthy, it was added to the Jungle Gardens collection and put on the market through his nursery. Several of these varieties, such as the Nina Avery, Virgin's Blush, and Cabeza de Vaca, remain widely admired and are still commercially available.

Black and white camellia images taken by noted photographer Harold Haliday Costain.

By the late 1930s, camellia nomenclature had become horribly muddled. Many camellias were known by three or four different names, while several different blooms bore the

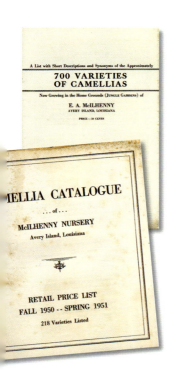

same name. McIlhenny decided to end this confusion. It was difficult, he discovered, to obtain recent information about camellias in English. He therefore translated and published at his own expense the *Nouvelle Iconographie des Camellias* by Alexandre Verschaffelt (thirteen volumes originally published in French between 1848–1860); and *The Monography of the Genus Camellia* by the Abbé Berlese (also originally published in French in 1838). McIlhenny placed these books on the market at a price he felt camellia enthusiasts could afford, believing the books would help to standardize the system used to identify camellias.

In 1941 McIlhenny put out a booklet cataloging his collection: *A List with Short Descriptions and Synonyms of the Approximately 700 Varieties of Camellias Now Growing in the Home Grounds (Jungle Gardens) of E. A. McIlhenny.* By this time, tens of thousands of camellia plants adorned Jungle Gardens. In 1950, a year after McIlhenny's death, the nursery published a camellia catalog that listed the correct names for 218 camellia varieties — eighteen of which originated in Jungle Gardens.

Lotus near Bird City, circa 1933.

"Interesting" PLANTS

The recent opening up of trade with Asia made plants from the Far East extremely fashionable. McIlhenny's botanical skills and the Gulf Coast's favorable climate allowed many desirable exotics to flourish on Avery Island. In 1921, McIlhenny compiled an inventory of these specimens. "The Following List Embraces a Few of the Interesting Plants Now Growing in Jungle Gardens," he wrote in a header, beneath which he recorded:

Aleurites fordii (tung-oil tree)

Diospyros kaki (Japanese persimmon)

Koelreuteria paniculata (golden rain tree)

Sapium sebiferum (Chinese tallow tree)

Podocarpus macrophylla (Japanese yew)

Bambusa alphonse karri and *Bambusa argentea striata* (bunching bamboos)

Phylostachys mitis (giant, edible bamboo)

Phyllostachys bambusoides (giant timber bamboo)

Camellia japonica

Azalea indica

Many of these plants are considered common or even "indigenous" today, but in fact even the camellia emigrated only recently to the US.

Despite McIlhenny's knowledge of local and exotic flora, correct plant identification was sometimes a challenge. The problem repeatedly frustrated McIlhenny and other horticulturists. Imported plant classifications were particularly confusing because names changed as botanists gathered more information about previously unknown varieties. McIlhenny received many specimens of the same plant under different names or several different plants under the same name. The USDA often sent "Correction of Plant Names" notices to growers, further complicating records. One of many planting notes left for McIlhenny by his gardeners observed: "The Hemerocallis (daylily) [named] J. R. Mann and Mrs. A. H. Austin are alike" as are "Mikado and Mirado." Such problems left McIlhenny and others puzzled about which names were correct and how to keep track of aliases.

Photo of Jungle Gardens camellias and palms by Harold Haliday Costain.

UNITED STATES DEPARTMENT OF AGRICULTURE
BUREAU OF ENTOMOLOGY AND PLANT QUARANTINE
~~BUREAU OF PLANT QUARANTINE~~
WASHINGTON, D. C.

March 7, 1936

Mr. E. A. McIlhenny,
Avery Island, La.

Dear Sir:

The plants imported by you under Special Permit No. 19375 have been received at Washington, D.C., and inspected under B. P. Q. No. A 34323

The number received was 10 Camellia reticulata

leaves have fallen

PERISHABLE — KEEP FROM HEAT

June 30, 1942

FROM U. S. Plant Introduction
COCONUT GROVE

To Mr. E. A. McIlhenny
Avery Island, Louisiana

STATE PLANT BOARD OF FLORIDA   NURSERY
Office of Nursery Inspector, Gainesville, Fla.

This is to certify that the nursery stock in the nursery of U. S. Plant Introduction Garden located at Coconut Grove, Florida has been inspected by an inspector of the State Plant Board in accordance with the Florida Plant Act of 1927 and the is believed to be free from all major plant pests; and has be other plant pests as to be entitled to movement under this in conformity to law and the rules and regulations of the Sta
This certificate is valid until June 30, 1942, unless revoked
Approved: WILMON NEWELL,
Plant Commissioner

"Void After"

DEC -5 1941

Rec'd from
US Plant Introduction
Coconut Grove Fla

one bale — 6 Plants

PI— 141978 — AGAPANTHUS AFRIC

Delevered to Pattenghouse

PLANT INTRODU

TWENTY-FOURT

ANNUAL DESCRIPTIV

Season 1935-6

Containing Descriptions of the More Important

Introduced Plants Now Ready

for Listed Experimenters

Division of Plant Exploration and Introduction

Bureau of Plant Industry

United States Department of Agriculture

Washington, D. C.

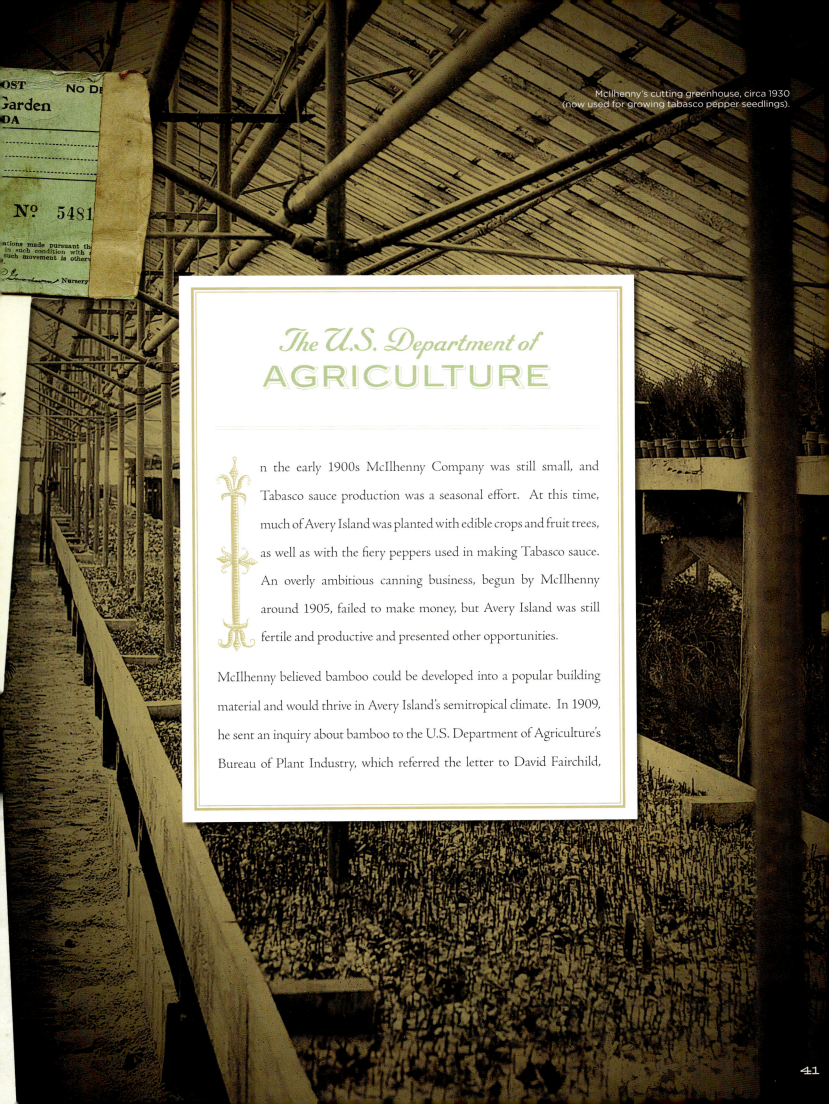

McIlhenny's cutting greenhouse, circa 1930 (now used for growing tabasco pepper seedlings).

The U.S. Department of AGRICULTURE

In the early 1900s McIlhenny Company was still small, and Tabasco sauce production was a seasonal effort. At this time, much of Avery Island was planted with edible crops and fruit trees, as well as with the fiery peppers used in making Tabasco sauce. An overly ambitious canning business, begun by McIlhenny around 1905, failed to make money, but Avery Island was still fertile and productive and presented other opportunities.

McIlhenny believed bamboo could be developed into a popular building material and would thrive in Avery Island's semitropical climate. In 1909, he sent an inquiry about bamboo to the U.S. Department of Agriculture's Bureau of Plant Industry, which referred the letter to David Fairchild, chief of the newly established Office of Foreign Seed and Plant Introduction. This office sent plant explorers[2] around the world to look for botanical specimens that would enhance the U.S. horticultural and agricultural markets. Many of these explorers were sent to China and other parts of Asia, which were newly opened to foreign trade. Very little information accompanied the plants and seeds brought to the United States, and the risk of introducing plant diseases and other horticultural threats was enormous and poorly understood at the time.

Fairchild's job included the coordination of plant explorer activity with acclimatization gardens in different regions of the country. When plants arrived in the US, the USDA relied on responsible growers to contain and nurse them back to health after long quarantines. Good records needed to be kept about the hardiness and potential advantages or problems of the plants. This information had to be relayed back to the USDA, along with healthy, successful specimens, if requested. Fairchild determined that McIlhenny's detailed knowledge of plants and his location on Avery Island would make him an effective experimental grower for the department.

Intending to foster a bamboo timber industry in south Louisiana, McIlhenny placed orders for bamboo from the USDA's Experimental Growers Catalog. It is clear that the increasing number of other exotic "Far East" plants becoming available through the USDA also intrigued him. He soon ordered other plants that he believed could have commercial value. At this time McIlhenny actively corresponded with Fairchild. These letters reveal McIlhenny's optimism and creativity about potentially useful items grown on Avery Island, as well as the polite but amused responses of an older and busy scientist. After Fairchild actually visited Avery Island, however, the two men enjoyed a more mutually admiring friendship.

During the spring of 1918, for instance, McIlhenny eagerly sent Fairchild an assortment of agricultural specimens that he hoped could be used commercially: Sugared figs,[3] fiber from a broad leaf palm, twenty-five pounds of dried okra pods, a living rhinoceros beetle,[4] a large quantity of dried grass. In response to the jumble of products and queries, Fairchild wrote back, "The trouble now, my dear McIlhenny, is that we have but two hands per person, and if you could find some way to make two persons grow where one person grew before, you would be doing a great service."[5]

Above, Postcard image of bamboo in Jungle Gardens, circa 1939.

Postcard image of bamboo in Jungle Gardens, circa 1939.

Magnificent BAMBOO

McIlhenny embraced the idea of bamboo as a valuable commodity. As he wrote in a promotional letter about Jungle Garden plants, "It is estimated by explorers that more than one-hundred-fifty-million people of the countries in Asia, bordering the Pacific Ocean, live in houses built entirely of bamboo."[6] He believed that both timber bamboo and edible shoot bamboo would be useful to Louisiana's economy and planted more than sixty-four varieties of bamboo in and around Jungle Gardens. His ability to observe and nurture plants made him the most successful bamboo experimenter in the country at that time. In 1918, McIlhenny confidently wrote Fairchild, "There can perhaps be taken a thousand plants [for distribution by the USDA] without hurting the grove."[7]

Jungle Gardens scene, circa 1940.

In 1946, McIlhenny wrote to the now retired Fairchild, outlining the status of his bamboo operations. McIlhenny pointed out that he was the nation's only commercial bamboo grower and that he was selling it successfully. "I am supplying practically all of the tuna poles to the Pacific Coast tuna fishing boats, and I am supplying large numbers of timber bamboos of the larger sizes for specific work."[8]

Although the US bamboo industry never flourished, McIlhenny's ability to see bamboo's potential and his success with a number of productive varieties astonished experts. Beverly Galloway, who took over the bamboo project at the USDA, wrote to McIlhenny

McIlhenny in grove of Moso bamboo, June 12, 1926.

McIlhenny with bambusa nana, a fine-leafed bamboo, circa 1922.

after reviewing his files, "It is interesting to note that of all the pioneer work done on bamboos, yours is outstanding. So far as bamboos are concerned, . . . [there is] no variety collection yet such as yours."⁹

Several types of bamboo still flourish in Jungle Gardens. The more interesting of these surviving varieties include a yellow bamboo with pale green stripes called Robert Young, located just before the Camellia Study Garden; impressively large Moso and Henon bamboos, found in a pretty grove near Bird City; and a small patch of Meyerii bamboo (named for an ill-fated plant explorer), which is quite tall and often very dark, almost black, growing to the left of the old entrance gate.

McIlhenny children in bamboo grove, 1934.

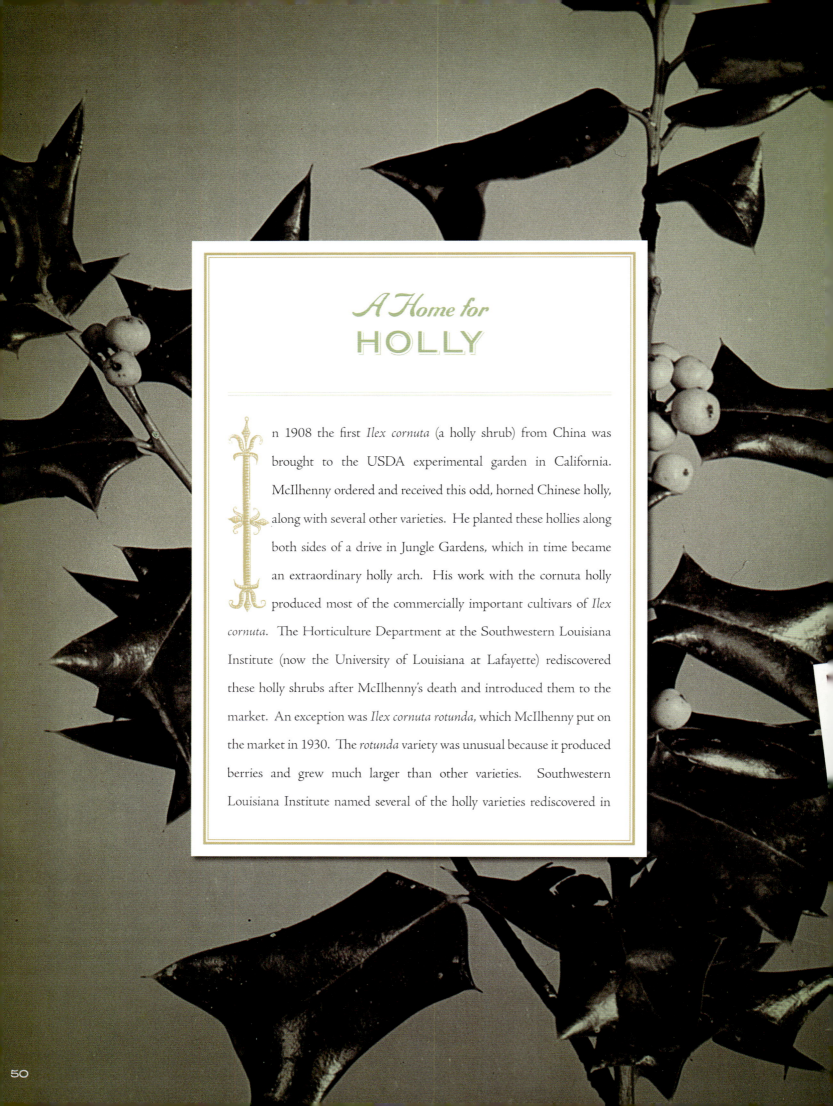

A Home for HOLLY

In 1908 the first *Ilex cornuta* (a holly shrub) from China was brought to the USDA experimental garden in California. McIlhenny ordered and received this odd, horned Chinese holly, along with several other varieties. He planted these hollies along both sides of a drive in Jungle Gardens, which in time became an extraordinary holly arch. His work with the cornuta holly produced most of the commercially important cultivars of *Ilex cornuta*. The Horticulture Department at the Southwestern Louisiana Institute (now the University of Louisiana at Lafayette) rediscovered these holly shrubs after McIlhenny's death and introduced them to the market. An exception was *Ilex cornuta rotunda*, which McIlhenny put on the market in 1930. The *rotunda* variety was unusual because it produced berries and grew much larger than other varieties. Southwestern Louisiana Institute named several of the holly varieties rediscovered in

Jungle Gardens for McIlhenny, Avery Island, Jungle Gardens, and McIlhenny's gardener, Anicet Delcambre. Most were found in the Gardens' Holly Arch and are still available from nurseries.

McIlhenny also grew *Ilex rotunda*. Unlike *Ilex cornuta rotunda*, it is a large tree with glossy, elliptical leaves and small, abundant, scarlet berries. Known as "Lord's Holly," it was popular in the late 1940s, but fell out of landscape use because of intolerance to cold. Four *Ilex rotunda* trees of about twenty to forty feet in height grow today in Jungle Gardens and represent some of the largest specimens of their kind.

Documentary photographs of Jungle Gardens hollies.

SECTION III: The FAUNA of JUNGLE GARDENS

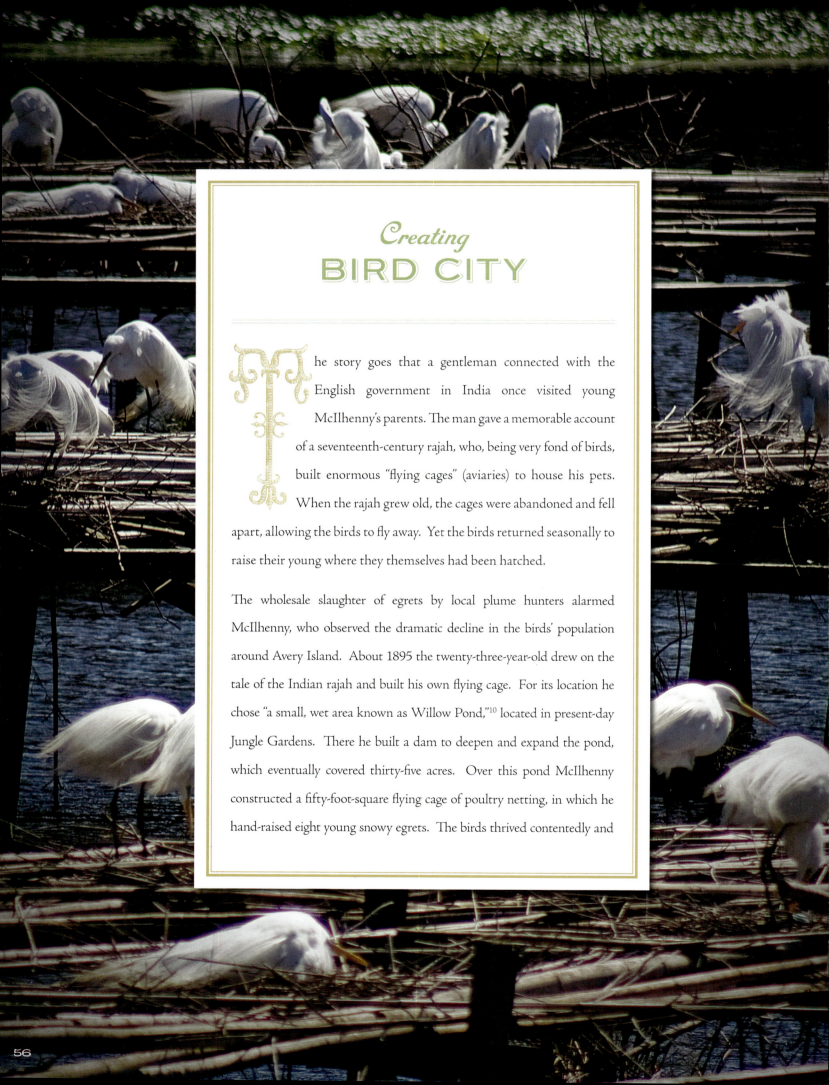

Creating
BIRD CITY

The story goes that a gentleman connected with the English government in India once visited young McIlhenny's parents. The man gave a memorable account of a seventeenth-century rajah, who, being very fond of birds, built enormous "flying cages" (aviaries) to house his pets. When the rajah grew old, the cages were abandoned and fell apart, allowing the birds to fly away. Yet the birds returned seasonally to raise their young where they themselves had been hatched.

The wholesale slaughter of egrets by local plume hunters alarmed McIlhenny, who observed the dramatic decline in the birds' population around Avery Island. About 1895 the twenty-three-year-old drew on the tale of the Indian rajah and built his own flying cage. For its location he chose "a small, wet area known as Willow Pond,"[10] located in present-day Jungle Gardens. There he built a dam to deepen and expand the pond, which eventually covered thirty-five acres. Over this pond McIlhenny constructed a fifty-foot-square flying cage of poultry netting, in which he hand-raised eight young snowy egrets. The birds thrived contentedly and

Previous spread,
Egrets nesting, 1930.

Left, Egrets on Bird City
nesting rack, 2008.

even seemed to enjoy interacting with their human keeper. As he fished on horseback for the egrets' food, noted McIlhenny, the birds would perch "fearlessly on my shoulders, head or arms and even on the neck of my horse, taking the food . . . from my hand, showing real pleasure in being with me."[11]

In the fall, McIlhenny freed his birds for their migration south. Early next March, as he hoped, six of his original eight birds returned to the flying cage, paired off, and hatched eight more chicks. This pattern continued and, sixteen years later, in March of 1911, McIlhenny estimated that one hundred thousand birds were nesting in what had

Postcard of egrets on Bird City nesting racks, circa 1939.

Left, McIlhenny captured and photographed the same bird specimens year after year to study how they changed over time.

Below, Metal bird bands from McIlhenny's files.

Bottom left, Colorized postcard of egrets, circa 1930.

[From 'The Auk,' Vol. LI, No. 3, July, 1934.]

NTY-TWO YEARS OF BANDING MIGRATORY WILD FOWL AT AVERY ISLAND, LOUISIANA.

BY E. A. McILHENNY.

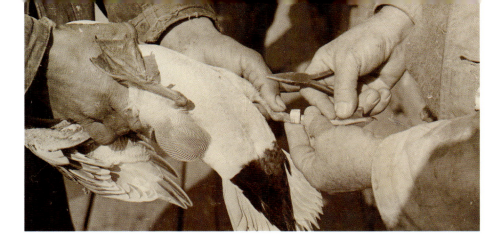

Bird banding, December 19, 1936.

become known as Bird City. The next year McIlhenny embarked on a massive bird-banding campaign, tagging over 285,000 birds by the 1940s. The data he collected provided significant insights into bird behavior and migration routes, and aided research conducted by the American Bird Banding Association. This project afforded McIlhenny a broader understanding of bird behavior and helped to make his refuge a balanced and successful one. Moreover, Bird City revived south Louisiana's egret population and provided a haven for many other wildfowl species. McIlhenny's efforts demonstrated that individuals could seize the initiative and make enormous advances in conservation. For this reason, Theodore Roosevelt, the father of American conservationism, called Bird City "the most noteworthy reserve in the country."[12]

McIlhenny banding birds, May 2, 1940.

Bird City nesting racks, circa 1940.

The Great ALLIGATOR

cIlhenny had observed alligators on Avery Island since childhood, when "seeing them was such an every-day occurrence that no unusual notice was taken of them by the children playing and swimming." Over the years he gathered much data about these large reptiles. In 1921, for example, McIlhenny discovered a female alligator laying eggs and kept meticulous notes about the process, recording the number of hatchlings and even marking the newborns for future observation. Ten years later, he came across one of these alligators as she built a nest of her own. McIlhenny

Right, Postcard of alligators in Jungle Gardens, circa 1968.

Below, Avery Island residents examine a captured alligator, circa 1900.

Alligator in Jungle Gardens, circa 1930.

Above, McIlhenny with alligator nest, circa 1930.

documented the construction method, noting that the mother built the nest with much green plant matter. He logged the daily temperature inside and outside the nest, discovering that warmth played a vital role in the eggs' incubation. Over time he came to understand that the green plant material broke down, and as it did so it generated heat that warmed the nest constantly and evenly. Furthermore, he noticed that the female alligator stood guard over the nest, responded to and assisted her young in the hatching process, and that the hatchlings remained under her protection for about a year. In 1935, McIlhenny published his findings in his book *The Alligator's Life History*,[13] which many zoologists still regard as the definitive study of alligator behavior. As famed biologist Archie Carr declared in the 1960s, "Old E. A. McIlhenny . . . was the first person to write about the fierce maternal behavior of alligators, back in 1935. He wasn't a trained zoologist. Nobody believed him. Reptiles weren't supposed to be maternal. But everything he said was right."[14]

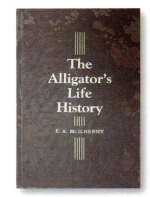

McIlhenny related the history and daily rituals of his wildfowl refuge in his book *Bird City*. In one passage, McIlhenny described his young grandsons and he seeing an alligator catch and eat an egret. The children asked why McIlhenny would allow alligators to be in Bird City. He explained that the alligators cruising around the frames of elevated nests actually kept most of the egrets safe at night. The birds could not see to protect themselves in the dark, he told them, and the alligators would much rather eat the fat raccoons, snakes, possums, and other predators that might try to raid the nests after dark. That was why the birds nested six feet above the water, to be safe from alligators and, at the same time, to benefit from the alligators' protection. He stressed to his grandchildren how the birds and alligators led interconnected lives, and how each depended on the other for survival.

McIlhenny constructed an alligator pen close to Willow Pond so that he could study alligator behavior in a controlled environment. "There were three of these pens with connecting doors between them. In two pens I kept large male alligators, in the third a large female."[15] McIlhenny monitored alligator mating behaviors and observed nesting females. The remains of one of McIlhenny's alligator pens can still be seen in Jungle Gardens near Bird City.

Visitors at alligator pen, Jungle Gardens, circa 1932.

Below, Large alligator caught in Jungle Gardens.

Above, Caricature depicting McIlhenny and his many interests, from the New Orleans *Times-Picayune*, May 21, 1917.

Other Birds & Animal CONSERVATION

Bird City serves as a refuge not only for the snowy egret, but for many other bird species. The spring brings songbirds to the protected area, and along with returning egrets come Louisiana herons and little blue herons. A little later arrive the night herons, least bitterns, and anhingas. Larger birds like the white ibises, roseate spoonbills, and great blue herons are more casual visitors, coming for a few days or just to rest a short time. Before the summer birds leave around August to migrate south, other species from the north begin to arrive. Blue-winged teals, pintails, and gadwalls show up first, followed by ducks, geese, coots and wading birds.

When McIlhenny found "winged" ducks — usually ducks wounded during hunting season — he placed them in the refuge to protect them. These birds often recovered, migrated, and returned to Bird City's safety the next fall and winter, just as egrets returned in spring and summer. In this way, Bird City became a year-round preserve for migratory birds. As McIlhenny wrote, "On one side of Bird City is a railroad track [now removed] and automobile road. The wild fowl that use this side do not mind the trains or automobiles or people walking along the road on foot, although they pass hourly within twenty feet of many ducks, without causing the birds to take wing. This is an excellent illustration of how friendly wild birds can become if protected, and given a chance to know man as a friend instead of a killer."[16]

Avery Island and the surrounding coastal marshlands support several large wild animal populations, including black bears. According to McIlhenny, he "possessed and raised as pets the young of almost every wild animal found [on Avery Island]."[17] His list included: deer, bears, wild cats, raccoons, opossums and snakes. All these animals still live on Avery Island, along with coyotes, armadillos, rabbits, otters, and muskrats, among many others. And while McIlhenny raised several bears from cubs as family pets, bears on the Island today are carefully managed and prevented from becoming too comfortable with people. After all, bear attacks and other nuisance behavior would threaten the specie's continued presence on the Island.

Right, Fawns nursing in Jungle Gardens, May 1940.

Left, Image of albino bird from McIlhenny's files.

The white-tailed deer was nearly hunted to extinction in the United States in the late 1800s. As a result, McIlhenny forbid deer hunting on Avery Island, and by 1925 the population of Island deer had stabilized. Biologists eventually recognized these deer as a new subspecies and named it *Odocoileus virginianus mcilhennyi* after McIlhenny, who supplied researchers with specimens and information about the deer and allowed them to collect additional data. In his 1902 book *The Deer Family*, Theodore Roosevelt quotes McIlhenny's older brother, John Avery McIlhenny — who during the Spanish-American War served with Roosevelt in the Rough Riders cavalry regiment — as a keen observer of the subspecies.

McIlhenny's interest in alligators did not preclude the study of other reptiles. He constructed a "terrapin crawl" in which he raised and bred diamondback terrapin, a kind of turtle that inhabited the local salt marshes. Many kinds of snapping turtles, mud turtles, and terrapin still reside in Jungle Gardens and along Bayou Petite Anse. Naturally, many types of frogs and toads live in the protected waters of Jungle Gardens, and sometimes they are extremely vocal.

Hoping to enhance the south Louisiana fur trade, McIlhenny used Jungle Gardens to raise nutria, a large rodent with red-orange teeth and magnificent fur. Imported to south Louisiana in the 1930s, nutria reproduced successfully and for decades were a boon to the state's fur industry. They eventually multiplied out of control, however, and inflicted much

damage on the coastal marshes. Feeding on wetlands grasses, nutria destroy the root system, which in turn permits soil to wash away and causes the marsh to become open water. McIlhenny has sometimes been blamed for single-handedly introducing nutria to Louisiana and even to the entire North American continent; but he never imported them from their native Argentina, as often claimed, nor was he the state's first nutria farmer. Regardless, Jungle Gardens, McIlhenny Company, and all of Avery Island's associated companies actively support and carry out coastal restoration projects today.

Left, above, Nutria in Jungle Gardens, 1940.

Far left, A nutria hat from the 1940s.

Right, Aerial photograph of Jungle Gardens, circa 1937.

Conservation, with its central tenet of man and nature in balance, was the cause to which McIlhenny most devoted himself. As he wrote, "Nature's teachings . . . are never tales. To those who understand her she speaks only truth. Her laws are just laws, and she shows no favoritism to any of her children."[18] McIlhenny served as the first president of the Audubon Society of Louisiana, which worked to protect wildfowl and their habitats.

Above, McIlhenny and his pet bear Billy Ballou, circa 1895.

Right, Harold Haliday Costain photograph of McIlhenny with his pet bear Tubby, February 18, 1934.

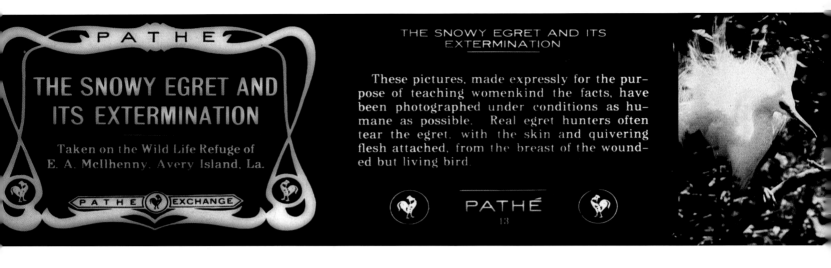

Above, Scenes from *The Snowy Egret and Its Extermination*, 1913.

Beginning around 1910, and with the help of several wealthy, conservation-minded friends and institutions — including northern businessman Charles Willis Ward, the heiress Mrs. Russell Sage, and the Rockefeller Foundation — McIlhenny oversaw the donation of about 175,000 acres of coastal wetlands to the state of Louisiana solely for wildfowl conservation. (Family lore holds that McIlhenny envisioned acquiring most of Louisiana's Gulf Coast as protected preserves.) In 1923 he and other investors bought 100,000 acres of land between the Rockefeller and Sage preserves and proposed setting up a seasonal hunting club on the land to fund year-round game wardens and wildlife management. The proposal failed, however, after more rigid conservationists decried the idea of hunting so closely to protected wildfowl preserves.

McIlhenny's curiosity about bird behavior and migration habits spurred him to join a national bird-banding campaign. He started to keep bird-banding records in January 1912, and by October 1942 he had banded 286,743 birds. He published his findings primarily in *The Auk*, an academic journal still published by the American Ornithologists' Union, and in *Bird-Banding*, now issued by the Association of Field Ornithologists. Around 1918 McIlhenny participated in a decades-long study of bird migration. He captured and banded birds, then shipped them to U.S. Biological Survey sites as far away as Oregon or New York for release. McIlhenny observed over and over again that significant numbers of banded birds returned to Avery Island, demonstrating that birds could find their way back to their original migration routes, even when released thousands of miles away from them.

In 1913 McIlhenny renewed his efforts to protect the snowy egret by commissioning the Pathé newsreel company to shoot *The Snowy Egret and Its Extermination*. Filmed

on Avery Island, the eight-minute silent movie featured stark images of plume hunters stalking, killing, and denuding egrets to obtain their long wispy feathers for women's hats. The violent scenes shocked early twentieth-century audiences, and the motion picture held female consumers responsible for the slaughter. As a film caption read, it condemned their "barbaric love of adornment that 1,800 years of Christian civilization has failed to eradicate."[19] McIlhenny exhibited the movie to the public at theaters, natural history museums, and ecological conferences. He even showed it on Capitol Hill to promote bird conservation measures. "We just ran out and brought the members of Congress in as we could catch them," McIlhenny recalled. "Once they saw that film, they were with us."

When in 1942 oil was found on Avery Island, McIlhenny allowed drilling, even in his beloved garden. But he required the oil companies to respect and coexist with

Right, 1962 chemical company advertisement that featured Jungle Gardens.

McIlhenny banding birds, May 2, 1940.

Right, McIlhenny hunting in November 1924.

Below, Oil derrick seen from Jungle Gardens, circa 1945.

the trees, plants, birds, and animals, and cause as little disruption as possible. When the drilling was done, McIlhenny saw to it that each leaseholder returned the site to its former state. Many of these oil companies used their relationships with McIlhenny and Avery Island to promote their brands as safe and conservation-minded. Today, this policy still holds true. All drilling and pumping is done with reverence for the Island and her inhabitants. Any landscape that is disturbed must be returned to its former condition before the oil, drilling, or mining company's obligation is discharged. In this way, Avery Island remains a resource for its people, as well as an example of harmony between man and the environment.

SECTION IV: The GARDENS of JUNGLE GARDENS

Previous spread, Bridge in the Buddha garden, 1937.
Below, McIlhenny in Jungle Gardens, circa 1920.

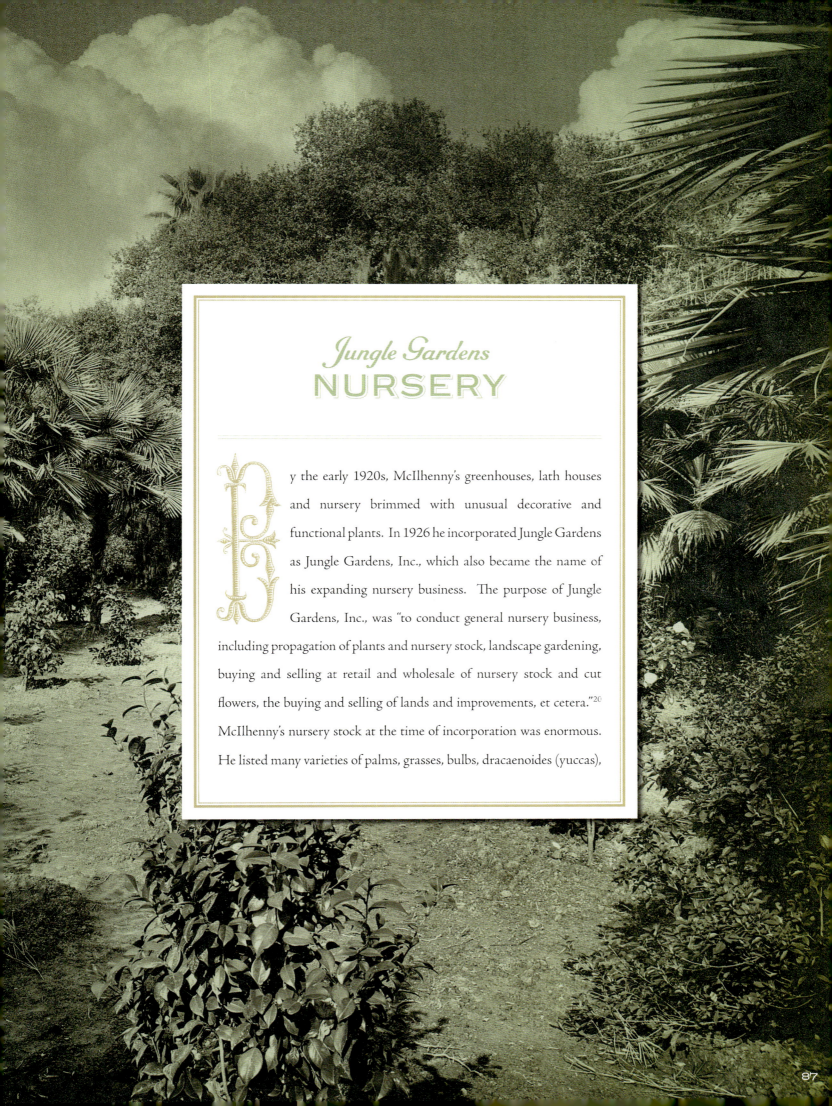

Jungle Gardens
NURSERY

By the early 1920s, McIlhenny's greenhouses, lath houses and nursery brimmed with unusual decorative and functional plants. In 1926 he incorporated Jungle Gardens as Jungle Gardens, Inc., which also became the name of his expanding nursery business. The purpose of Jungle Gardens, Inc., was "to conduct general nursery business, including propagation of plants and nursery stock, landscape gardening, buying and selling at retail and wholesale of nursery stock and cut flowers, the buying and selling of lands and improvements, et cetera."[20] McIlhenny's nursery stock at the time of incorporation was enormous. He listed many varieties of palms, grasses, bulbs, dracaenoides (yuccas),

JUNGLE GARDENS NURSERY
SPECIALIST IN SOUTHERN LANDSCAPE STOCK
AVERY ISLAND, LA.

1926
Plants in home grounds of EAM

OUR ORDER NO.
CONSIGNED TO
VIA

VARIETY	SIZE	PRICE EACH	AMOUNT	TOTAL

Aesculus pavia (Red Buckeye)
Agave americana
Agapanthus multiflorus
Agave marginata
Alocasia odorata (tree elephant ear)
Alstroemeria pulchella (parrot plant)
Aleuritis fordii
Amorpha fruticosa (purple upright spike near pond small tree)
Araucaria bidwillie (below my house)
Ardesia crennlata
Arundo donax variegata
Alpinia mutica (growth like ginger lily)
Accacia cornigera (bull thorn on side of hill)
Callistemon lanceolatus (bottle brush)
Catalpa ovata japonica (in old garden)
Catha edulis
Celtis mississippiansis (hackberry)
Cercis chinensis
Chaenomelis japonica (jap quince)
Cinnamomum zeylanicum
Clematis paniculata
Clerodendron foetidum
Cocculus laurifolia
Colocasia euchlora (small black green)
Cleome spinosa (spider plant)
Colocasia fontanesii (many runners)
Colocasia antiquorum
Colocasia illustris (black)
Cryptomeria japonica (near hackberry)
Curculigo latifolia
Cycas revoluta
Cyperus papyrus
Cyperus alternifolius (umbrella plant)
Cordyline terminalis (green dracaena)
Cordyline australis (fine leaf dracaena)
Dasylirion texanum
Phoenix dactylifera (date palm)
Datura suaveolens
Dioscorea bulbifera (air potato)
Diospyras virginiana
Diospyras kaki
Erythrina crista-galli
Erythrina herbacea (native)
Escallonia leucantha
Escallonia beteriana
Eucalyptus rostrata
Eugenia unifloria (surinam cherry)
Fatsia papyrifera arralia
Ficus pumila (ripens)
Fraxinus americana (white ash)
Gardenia jasmonides (small)
Ginkgo biloba
Grevillea robusta (silk oak)
Ipomoea digitata (tuberous morning glory)
Ipomoea pandurata (native white)
Jacobinia carnea (not justicia)
Jasminum revolutum (large leaf bush yellow)
Jasminum pumila (small leaf bush)
Jasminum officinale (white star bush) (Persia
Jasminum primilinum (China)
Jasminum nudiflorum (China)
Jasminum Sambac (Grand Duke)(India)
Jasminum grandiflorum (India (near pond)
Kerria japonica (China) near pond (single)
Kerria flore-Plen - double
Lespedeza sieboldii (pink)
Lespedeza japonica (white)

One of the propagating hous in which the cuttings of Jungle Gardens plants are grown. This house has a capacity of 750,000

JUNGLE GARDENS,
SPECIALIST IN SOUTHERN LANDSCAPE STOC
AVERY ISLAND, LA.

ADDRESSES:
TELEGRAPH,
NEW IBERIA, LA.
EXPRESS AND FREIGHT,
AVERY ISLAND, LA.

SOLD TO
TERMS
QUANTITY
OUR O
CONSI
VIA
VARIETY
SIZE

One of the lath sheds in which Azaleas, Aspidistras and shade loving plants are grown.

"shade trees (not evergreens)," conifers, evergreen trees, evergreen shrubs, "vines (evergreen)," "shrubs (not evergreen)," hardy perennials, soft-wooded evergreens, and bamboos, among others. At one time Jungle Gardens, Inc., grew plants in the tens of thousands and boasted six thousand acres of land, some on Avery Island, but most of it just off the Island. Today, Jungle Gardens no longer operates as a nursery and covers only 170 acres, including Bird City and the exhibition gardens that served as McIlhenny's experimental nursery.

The Jungle Gardens, Inc., nursery business spun off two branches from the Avery Island office, and attracted many wholesale agents. Ralph Ellis Gunn, a prominent landscape architect who worked on the River Oaks area of Houston, operated Jungle Gardens' successful Houston office, located at the present-day site of the Galleria Mall. Gunn and wife Esme were McIlhenny family favorites and often visited Avery Island. A friend of McIlhenny's daughters, Dorothy Thomas Penick, ran Jungle Gardens' other satellite nursery, located at 1530 Clio Street in New Orleans.

The reputation of Jungle Gardens, Inc., as an unusual nursery attracted many sizeable projects. In response, McIlhenny hired landscape architects to help with designs for his clients. Perhaps the most noteworthy of these landscape architects was A. A. Hunt, a

Jungle Gardens and Bird City, circa 1930.

AGENT'S MONTHLY REPORT OF SALES FOR ACCOUNT OF E. A. McILHENNY "PLANTS FOR THE SOUTH" AVERY ISLAND, LOUISIANA								
REPORT OF Chas. Corkern, Agent Address Bogalusa, La.				REPORT No. Page 3 FOR MONTH ENDING Feb. 28, 1938				
VARIETY	Number on Hand From Last Report	Number Received Since Last Report	Total Number To Account For	Number Dead	Number Sold	Price Each	Total Value Plants Sold	Balance on H
Salix elegantissima	3 ✓		3			1 00		
Thuya baker	8 ✓		8			1 50		8
" aurea nana	2 ✓		2			2 50		
" " "	5 ✓		5			1 25		
Viburnum suspensum	6 ✓		6			75		
" japonica	5 ✓		5		1	50	1 50	
Vitex agnus	3 ✓		3			1 25		3
Weigelia rosea	5 ✓		5			75		5
Roses—Pink radiance	2 ✓		2			35		2

Yucca and spirea in Jungle Gardens, circa 1935.

New state capitol grounds, landscaped by Jungle Gardens, Inc., Baton Rouge, circa 1932.

British landscape engineer who had previously worked at the Royal Botanical Gardens at Kew and who served as an original Jungle Gardens, Inc., board member. Hunt went on to work at Bellingrath Gardens in Alabama and oversaw many of the camellia gardens there. In his 1935 resignation letter, Hunt confessed to McIlhenny, "Possibly no one will ever know what Avery Island, Jungle Gardens, Inc., and its associations have meant, and still mean to me. It absorbed all I had to offer, both mental and physical."[21]

Throughout the 1920s and early 1930s, Jungle Gardens, Inc., continued to cultivate, experiment with, and accumulate interesting plants, and McIlhenny persisted in his search for outlets for his stock. The Jungle Gardens nursery undertook numerous landscaping projects, most notably those for the old and new state capitol buildings in Baton Rouge. The Gardens provided plants for other big projects, such as Louisiana State University's main campus, City Park in New Orleans, the Bayou Bend estate in Houston, and many other private residential gardens. On Avery Island itself, McIlhenny's landscaped areas exhibited architectural and design elements that he sometimes copied for his clients. For example, in New Orleans' City Park he replicated the bridge from his Buddha temple garden.

Although McIlhenny and his team were capable of creating formal gardens, they preferred to design modified natural settings. McIlhenny's structured projects in the Gardens served as more than mere canvases for his plants. By controlling the flow of rainwater, he ingeniously turned a problematic gully into the lush Sunken Garden. A disused sand pit became the Cactus or Palm Garden. He fashioned a walled rock garden to preserve a live oak threatened by hillside erosion. Some present-day Jungle Gardens sights are actually vestigial elements from its earlier days as a working plant nursery. For example, striking though wildly overgrown rows of camellias and evergreens can be found in the Gardens' more remote areas. Many of these forgotten, untended camellias have grown up to 20 feet in height, an unexpected scale for such a familiar Louisiana denizen.

Jungle Gardens, Inc., truck at new state capitol building, Baton Rouge, circa 1932.

Opening to THE PUBLIC

To encourage automobile tourism, McIlhenny quietly opened Jungle Gardens to the "motoring" public in 1935. He believed this relatively new form of tourism would stimulate Depression-era commerce and spur the construction of better roads, a goal partly achieved already by charismatic Louisiana governor Huey P. Long. National articles promoted tourism to Avery Island, and particularly to Jungle Gardens. McIlhenny advertised with motoring clubs and cooperated with publications aimed at automobile enthusiasts. "Graveled roads make it possible to drive comfortably about the gardens," noted one of these journals, *ESSO Road News*, in 1936. Avery Island's remoteness and the Gardens' growing reputation as a tourism destination — coupled with America's newfound interest in automobiles — made a drive-through garden extremely attractive. Tourists came by the thousands to see the beautiful setting, exotic plants, and bird refuge.

Views of Jungle Gardens, circa 1935.

McIlhenny grafting oranges, circa 1920.

Kettle pool postcard, circa 1935.

WASE ORANGE

Many people discovered Jungle Gardens and McIlhenny's botanical activities through his satellite nurseries, through hunting parties hosted on his wide expanse of marshland, or through the USDA. The beauty and scale of the Avery Island garden astounded most visitors. Able to weave a story when required, McIlhenny bewitched and charmed his guests with increasingly colorful accounts of the origins of his plants. Told in such an exotic landscape, McIlhenny's stories made him and his gardens particularly intriguing.

One of the more colorful stories McIlhenny told about the gardens concerned the Wase orange. He would escort visitors through his citrus groves and stop at a small, unassuming tree and tell of how once in the Arctic he rescued a member of Japan's imperial family. The emperor was so grateful he sent McIlhenny one of his Wase orange trees, usually reserved only for the emperor himself.

The origins of the little tree were perhaps somewhat overstated: The wase does exist as a variety of early ripening satsuma, and McIlhenny did help to rescue a marooned Japanese sailor named Jujiro Wada, son of a once-prominent Japanese samurai; but the rest of the story is questionable. Regardless, the tale entranced visitors and was retold numerous times in newspapers and other media outlets.

Above, below, Postcards of Jungle Gardens views, circa 1935.

Left, Holly arch in Jungle Gardens.

Embracing BUDDHA

A year after Jungle Gardens opened to the public, two of McIlhenny's friends, Robert M. Youngs and Ernest B. Tracy of New York City, discovered a magnificent Buddha statue in a Manhattan warehouse. Its provenance was vague: It had apparently been in storage for some time, unclaimed, and opinions varied about its origin. Some asserted that the statue had been commissioned by the twelfth-century emperor Hui-Tsung (1101-1125), created by artist Chon-Ha-Chin, and taken from the Shonfa Temple near Peking by a rogue Chinese warlord. Purchasing the statue, Youngs and Tracy presented the relic to McIlhenny, hoping it would find a suitable home among the Asian flora of his gardens. When the Buddha finally arrived on Avery Island, McIlhenny immediately thanked Youngs and Tracy, saying that he

Right, McIlhenny and Buddha statue, circa 1936.

Left, Buddha temple in Jungle Gardens, circa 1950.

Right, below, Buddha garden views from 1935 to present.

Left, Japanese torii gate at Buddha garden, circa 1940.

would find a worthy and permanent place in his garden for the statue. "As it is of wood," he added, "it will have to have a temple especially prepared for it."[22]

McIlhenny chose a location and set about building a garden for the Buddha statue. Next to a lagoon he constructed a rocky mound topped with a small Asian temple in a bamboo motif. Inside the temple he placed the statue atop a lotus blossom pedestal of wood and copper. McIlhenny landscaped the surrounding area using many of his more beautiful and rare Asian plants. He built seven "sacred hills," each about ten feet in height, to complement the temple, and he planted each of these knolls with Chinese azalea. Finally, he erected an arched stone bridge over the lagoon and lined the banks with Chinese iris, making a placid reflecting pool for the temple. The result was a lovely and serenely exotic garden for the statue.

Below, Japanese torii gate and china elephants at steps to Buddha temple.

The Buddha quickly became a focal point for visitors. In recent years, the Gardens has served as an active place of worship for local Buddhists. They conduct several ceremonies there during the year, most notably on the Buddha's birthday.

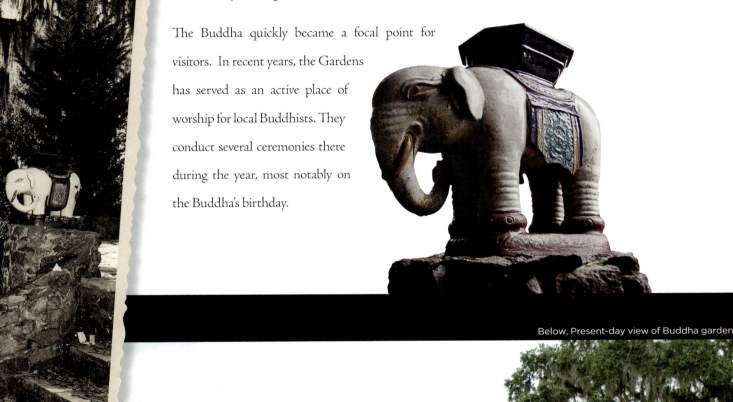

Below, Present-day view of Buddha garden.

Left, Buddha temple under construction, circa 1936.
Below left, McIlhenny poem on plaque at Buddha temple.

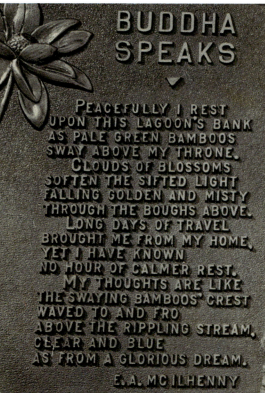

BUDDHA SPEAKS

Peacefully I rest
upon this lagoon's bank
as pale green bamboos
sway above my throne.
Clouds of blossoms
soften the sifted light
falling golden and misty
through the boughs above.
Long days of travel
brought me from my home,
yet I have known
no hour of calmer rest.
My thoughts are like
the swaying bamboos' crest
waved to and fro
above the rippling stream,
clear and blue
as from a glorious dream.

E. A. McIlhenny

Right, McIlhenny standing on future site of Buddha temple, circa 1936.

Jungle Gardens after E. A. McILHENNY

In 1946 McIlhenny suffered a stroke from which he never completely recovered. His daughter, Pauline "Polly" McIlhenny Simmons, assisted him by overseeing Jungle Gardens, answering correspondence, and administering other business matters. On McIlhenny's death in 1949, Simmons took over the operation of Jungle Gardens. She kept the Gardens open to the public, but greatly reduced the nursery business, selling only bamboo and camellias. She was instrumental in sorting out the issue of camellia identification and published her results in the Gardens' 1950–51 camellia catalog, which correctly listed the 18 varieties originated by her father. Simmons capably ran Jungle Gardens until her death in 1980, when her son, Edward McIlhenny Simmons, assumed leadership. He reorganized the corporation, allowing Jungle Gardens to operate autonomously and independently, as it does today.

Jungle Gardens gently entered a quiescent state after McIlhenny's death. Today, no experimentation takes place, and no plants are sold. New plantings serve primarily as replacements for azaleas, camellias, and oaks that have been damaged by time or weather. New interest has developed

Right, Pauline "Polly" McIlhenny Simmons and her son, Edward McIlhenny Simmons, 1965.

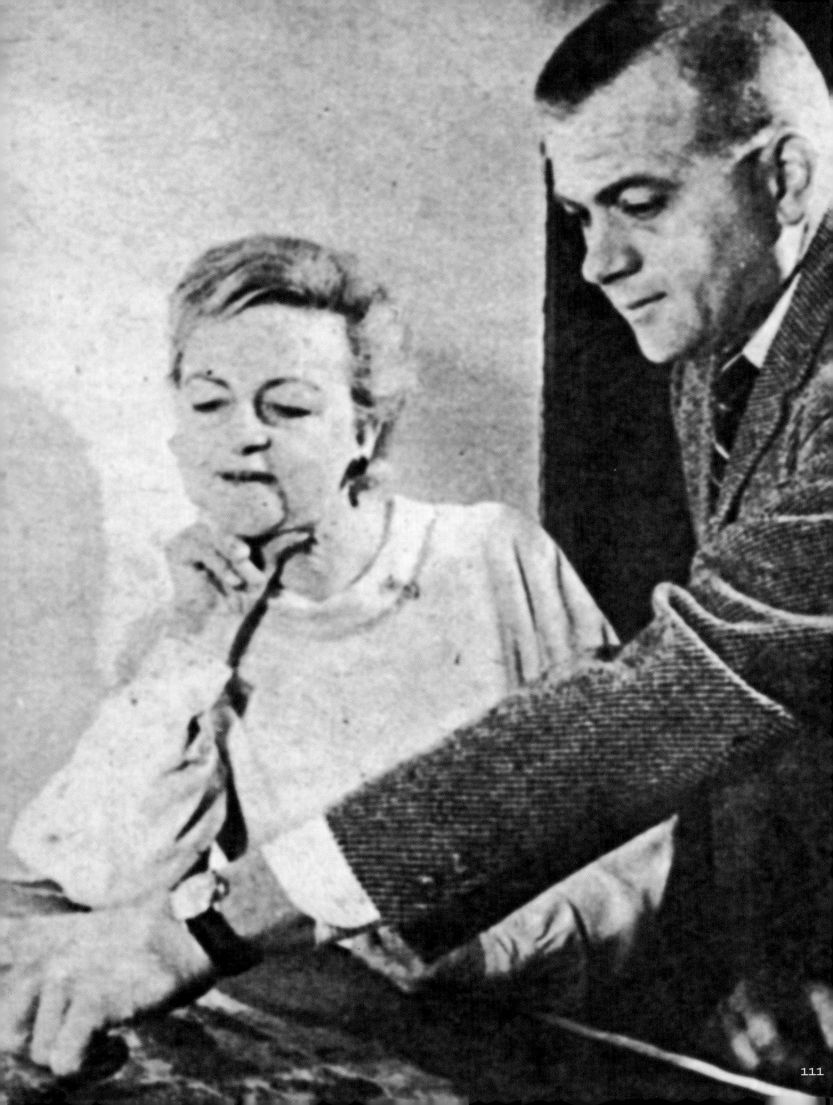

in the bamboo groves, however, which are cleared and cared for in late-winter by teams of bamboo enthusiasts. The passage of time and the shifting of priorities have clouded much knowledge about the trees and plants in the gardens, including their proper identification. Scientific names changed during McIlhenny's lifetime and have certainly changed since his death. Some plants have been lost, but others thrive, protected by their hidden identities. Man's activities have further reduced bird populations, although thousands still find refuge in the Gardens today. Always much more than a pretty park, Jungle Gardens quietly continues to hold many extraordinary secrets.

In his introduction to McIlhenny's book *Bird City*, author Harris Dickson[23] wrote that McIlhenny's realm "is sufficient unto itself. If a Chinese wall was built around him, shutting him off from all mankind . . . McIlhenny could snap his fingers at the world and live like a prince, for his soil and waters will supply his needs." Dickson illustrated this point by listing some of the things McIlhenny produced on Avery Island, including in Jungle Gardens: He grew his own coffee, tea, sugar, grapefruits, oranges, papayas, avocados, guavas, tangerines, kumquats, peaches, figs, and mushrooms, and from the woods, wetlands, and Gulf of Mexico he obtained bass, perch, oysters, shrimp, crab, duck, venison, turkey, bear, and turtle. McIlhenny's table, continued Dickson, could be decorated with camellias, roses, azaleas, or other exotic flowers, but all of this bounty came from a fertile mind as well as fertile ground.

McIlhenny had the ability, observed the author, to see the land's potential and to realize it. As Dickson concluded, "Other men live in the same climate on soil that is just as fertile, yet buy their rations of meat and meal from a grocery store in town." Through his understanding of nature and the land, McIlhenny protected and fortified his resources, and lived a generous, creative life. A friend of McIlhenny's wrote about the "aura of enchantment" that he created in Jungle Gardens, adding, "I went back to visit the Gardens once after Mr. McIlhenny's death, and while the same plants were still beautiful, the touch of magic his presence gave was gone, and the place seemed to me much like the body of a lovely lady from which the soul had departed."[24]

Jungle Gardens is only part of the life and legacy of E. A. McIlhenny. He had an ability to make the most of opportunities presented to him. His many efforts did not always prove wise or successful, but McIlhenny rarely left a prospect unexplored. He attempted

Sugi or temple cypress tree near Bird City in Jungle Gardens.

many things and achieved a few exceptional feats. "Do what you can, with what you have, where you are," said Theodore Roosevelt, whom McIlhenny admired — and McIlhenny did precisely that. McIlhenny was a man able to see beyond himself and his time. His efforts still benefit the people and wildlife of Louisiana. He continues, more than half a century after his death, to have a profound effect on his family — though many are too young to have known him — and on Avery Island, where his influence lingers both in the landscape and in the ecology of present-day inhabitants.

"Let those who would live happily and approach the inevitable with a peaceful mind, take heed to nature's teachings: live a natural life; watch, listen and think; for the more of these three things you do the sooner you will realize that your happy, natural fate, lies solely in yourself and your life on earth, and not in the future."

— E. A. McIlhenny

B-18 JUNGLE GARDENS AT AVE.

ABOUT THE AUTHORS

Lisa B. Osborn is the great-granddaughter of Jungle Gardens founder E. A. McIlhenny. A sculptor, she attended Boston University and holds a Master of Fine Arts degree from the Massachusetts College of Art in Boston. Osborn has exhibited her artwork extensively, served for several years as a Visiting Lecturer at Harvard University, and now resides on Avery Island, Louisiana.

Shane K. Bernard serves as historian and curator to the McIlhenny Company and Avery Island, Inc., Archives. He holds degrees in English and History from the University of Louisiana at Lafayette and a doctorate in History from Texas A&M University. He is the author of several books, including *The Cajuns: Americanization of a People* (2004) and *Tabasco: An Illustrated History* (2007).

Scott Carroll is a graphic designer who in 1995 opened his own design studio in New Orleans after a time with a small advertising agency. A native of St. Louis, Missouri, Carroll attended Loyola University in New Orleans where he obtained his BA degree in Graphic Arts and taught part-time after he graduated. Carroll's versatility as a designer allows him to work on a gambit of projects ranging from logo and package designs to advertising campaigns to books and annual reports. Carroll resides in Metairie, Louisiana, with his wife and two daughters.

Postcard of water gardens near Bird City, Jungle Gardens, circa 1930.

INDEX

A. H. Austin (daylily), 38.
Alligator's Life History, The (book), 68.
Alligators, 66-69.
American Bird Banding Association, 61.
American Ornithologists' Union, 78.
Arctic exploration, 25, 27, 99.
Association of Field Ornithologists, 78.
Audubon Society, 76.
Auk, The (journal), 78.
Automobile tourism, 94.
Avery Island, Louisiana, conservation on, 79, 82; crops grown on, 41, 113; environmental motto of, 19; home of Tabasco sauce, 41; oil production on, 79, 82; wildlife on, 73-75.
Bamboo, 41, 42, 45-49, 113.
Baton Rouge, Louisiana, 92.
Bears, 74.
Bellingrath Gardens, Alabama, 92.
Berlese, Abbé, 35.
Bird banding, 61, 78.
Bird-Banding, The (journal), 78.
Bird City (book), 69, 113.
Bird City, as home to various bird species, 73; early growth of, 59, 61; origin of, 56; praised by Theodore Roosevelt, 61.
Birds, 56-61, 73-74, 78-79.
Black bears, 74.
Buddha statue, 100-105.
Bureau of Plant Industry, 41.
Cabeza de Vaca (camellia), 34.
Camellia reticulata, 34.
Camellia sasanqua, 34.
Camellias, 31-35, 93, 110.
Carr, Archie, 68.
Chon-Ha-Chin, 100.
City Park (New Orleans), 92.
Civil War, U.S., 31, 34.
Cook, Frederick, 25.
Daylily, 38.
Deer, 75.
Delcambre, Anicet, 53.
Dickson, Harris, 113.
Egrets, 56-61.
Fairchild, David, 41-42, 45, 46.
Frogs, 75.
Fur industry, 75-76.
Galloway, Beverly, 46, 49.
Governor Mouton (camellia), 34.
Greenland, 25.
Hemerocallis, 38.
Henon (bamboo), 49.
Holly (plant), 50-53.
Houston, Texas, 89, 92.
Hui-Tsung, 100.
Hunt, A. A., 89, 92.
Hunting, 73, 99.
Ilex cornuta (holly), 50.
Ilex cornuta rotunda (holly), 50, 53.
Ilex rotunda, 53.
J. R. Mann (daylily), 38.
Jungle Gardens, as plant introduction garden, 37-38, 41-42; as plant nursery, 87-93; as site of Bird City wildfowl refuge, 56-61; as tourism destination, 94; Cactus Garden, 93; Camellia Study Garden, 49; Holly Arch, 53; list of plants growing in, 37; location of, 15; origin of, 18, 21; Palm Garden, 93; purpose of, 18, 19; size of, 15, 89; reorganization, 110; Sunken Garden, 93; wildlife in, 73-75.
Long, Governor Huey P., 94.
Lord's Holly, 53.
Louisiana black bears, 74.
Louisiana State University, 92.
McIlhenny (Simmons), Pauline "Polly," 110.
McIlhenny Company, 27, 41, 76.
McIlhenny, Edmund, 21.
McIlhenny, Edward Avery, and bird banding, 61, 78; and conservation, 76, 78, 79, 82; and nutria, 76; arctic exploration, 25, 27, 99; as first president of Audubon Society of Louisiana, 76; as nurseryman, 87-93; as ornithologist, 25; as storyteller, 99; as wild pet owner, 74; assumes presidency of McIlhenny Company, 27; caricature of, 72; childhood interest in nature, 21, 23; clarifies plant taxonomy, 35, 113, 38; correspondence and friendship with David Fairchild, 42, 45; death of, 35, 110; deer subspecies named for, 75; donation of marshland to state of Louisiana as wildfowl refuges, 78; encourages automobile tourism, 94; films *The Snowy Egret and Its Extermination*, 23, 78-79; founds Bird City, 56; friendship with Charles Willis Ward, 78; interest in alligators, 66-69; interest in bamboo, 41-42, 45, 46; interest in biology, 25; interest in egrets, 56-61; interest in holly, 50; legacy of, 113-14; plants named after, 50-51; receives Buddha statue, 100-105; rediscovers and collects camellias, 34; self-sufficiency of, 113; starts family, 27; translates camellia books, 35.
McIlhenny, John Avery, 75.
McIlhenny, Mary Eliza Avery, 20, 27.
Meyerii (bamboo), 49.
Mikado (daylily), 38.
Mirado (daylily), 38.
Miranda (ship), 25.
Monography of the Genus Camellia, The (book), 35.
Moso (bamboo), 49.
Mouton, Governor Alexandre, 34.
New Orleans, Louisiana, 89, 92.
Nidologist, The (magazine), 25.
Nina Avery (camellia), 34.
Nouvelle Iconographie des Camellias (book), 35.
Nursery, Jungle Gardens as, 87-93.
Nutria, 75-76.
Odocoileus virginianus mcilhennyi, 75.
Office of Foreign Seed and Plant Introduction, 42.
Oil, production on Avery Island, 79, 82.
Oranges, 99.
Ornithology, 25.
Pathé newsreel company, 78-79.
Peking, China, 100.
Penick, Dorothy Thomas, 89.
Petroleum, production on Avery Island, 79, 82.
Plant exploration, 42.
Plant taxonomy, 38.
Plume hunters, 23, 56, 79.
Point Barrow, Alaska, 25, 27.
Ralph Ellis Gunn, 89.
Refuges, 78.
Robert Young (bamboo), 49.
Rockefeller Foundation, 78.
Roosevelt, Theodore, 61, 75, 114.
Sage, Mrs. Russell, 78.
Shonfa Temple, China, 100.
Simmons, Edward McIlhenny, 110.
Simmons, Pauline "Polly" McIlhenny, 110.
Snowy Egret and Its Extermination, The (film), 23, 78-79.
Southwestern Louisiana Institute, 50.
Tabasco sauce, 27, 41.
Tourism, 94.
Tracy, Ernest B., 100.
Turtles, 75.
United States Department of Agriculture (USDA), 41-42, 45, 46, 50.
University of Louisiana at Lafayette, 50.
Vedrine (camellia), 34.
Verschaffelt, Alexandre, 35.
Vidrine, Louisiana, 24.
Virgin's Blush (camellia), 34
Wada, Jujiro, 99.
Ward, Charles Willis, 78.
Wase oranges, 99.
White-tailed deer, 75.
Wildfowl refuges, 78.
Willow Pond, 27, 56, 69.
Youngs, Robert M., 100.

ENDNOTES

1. John Bockstoce, "The Arctic Whaling Disaster of 1897," *Prologue: The Journal of the National Archives* (Spring 1977): 27–42.

2. As the National Agricultural Library observes, "Honored the world over for his contributions as a plant explorer, Frank Meyer's work touches us all everyday. From apricots to wild pears, his introductions number over 2,500." Born in the Netherlands, Meyer (1875-1918) traveled to Asia several times as a plant explorer for the USDA. His final trip to China occurred from 1916 to 1918, when he searched out edible and timber bamboos, tung-oil trees, tallow trees, root crops for wetlands, and ornamental shrubs, among other plants. During that trip, however, Meyer fell overboard and drowned in the Yangtze River. Although his body was recovered, circumstances surrounding his death remain a mystery. Several Frank Meyer introductions grow in Jungle Gardens.

    See http://www.nalusda.gov/speccoll/collectionsguide/collection.php?subject=Plant_Exploration

3. David Fairchild passed the figs around and received many favorable replies. One response came from famed Washington journalist Frank B. Noyes, who stated that his family and he liked the figs very much and that he had "read accounts of the bird refuge on [McIlhenny's] place." David Fairchild, Washington, D.C., to E. A. McIlhenny, Avery Island, La., 5 August 1918, TLS, E. A. McIlhenny Collection, Hill Memorial Library, Louisiana State University, Baton Rouge, La.

4. Fairchild and his wife, Marion (daughter of Alexander Graham Bell), photographed bugs at close range and published the images as *Book of Monsters* (Washington, D.C.: National Geographic Society, 1914).

5. David Fairchild, Washington, D.C., to E. A. McIlhenny, Avery Island, La., 1 May 1918, TLS, E. A. McIlhenny Collection, Avery Island, La.

6. E. A. McIlhenny, Letter to Agents, [1927?], E. A. McIlhenny Collection, Avery Island, La.

7. E. A. McIlhenny, [Avery Island, La.], to David Fairchild, [Washington, D.C.], 10 January 1918, TL, E. A. McIlhenny Collection, Hill Memorial Library, Louisiana State University, Baton Rouge, La.

8. E. A. McIlhenny, [Avery Island, La.], to David Fairchild, [Washington, D.C.], 30 October 1946, TL, E. A. McIlhenny Collection, Avery Island, La.

9. Beverly T. Galloway, Washington, D.C., to E. A. McIlhenny, Avery Island, La., 3 May 1926, TLS, E. A. McIlhenny Collection, Hill Memorial Library, Louisiana State University, Baton Rouge, La.

    For further information about E. A. McIlhenny and bamboo on Avery Island, see Andrew D. Ringle, "Edward Avery McIlhenny: Pioneer Bamboo Planter," Louisiana-Gulf Coast Chapter of the American Bamboo Society, http://www.lgcc-abs.org/DF/McIlhenny_History.pdf

10. E. A. McIlhenny, *Bird City* (Boston: Christopher Publishing House, 1934), 122–23.

11. Ibid., 123.

12. Theodore Roosevelt, "The Bird Refuges of Louisiana," *Scribner's Magazine*, March 1916, 280.

13. E. A. McIlhenny wrote several books and articles. For a complete list, see the Appendix.

14. Quoted in David Ehrenfeld, *Beginning Again: People and Nature in the New Millennium* (New York: Oxford University Press, 1993), 4.

15. E. A. McIlhenny, *The Alligator's Life Story* (Boston, Mass.: Christopher Publishing House, 1935), 90.

16. McIlhenny, *Bird City*, 187–88.

17. E. A. McIlhenny, "Nature Ramblings," Number 91, E. A. McIlhenny Collection, Avery Island, La.

18. McIlhenny, *Bird City*, 4.

19. Caption from E. A. McIlhenny, *The Snowy Egret and Its Extermination*, silent motion picture (New York: Pathé Frères, 1913).

20. Articles of Incorporation (1926), Clerk of Court's Office, Iberia Parish Courthouse, New Iberia, La.

21. A. A. Hunt, Mobile, Ala., to E. A. McIlhenny, [Avery Island, La.], 25 August 1935, ALS, E. A. McIlhenny Collection, Avery Island, La.

22. E. A. McIlhenny, Avery Island, La., to Robert W. Youngs, New York, N.Y., 5 June 1936, TL, E. A. McIlhenny Collection, Avery Island, La.

23. Harris Dickson in McIlhenny, *Bird City*, 9-10.

24. Joel L. Fletcher, "E. A. McIlhenny: The Most Interesting Man I Ever Knew," Syllabus for Louisiana Education 341, 1956, Southwestern Louisiana Institute (University of Louisiana at Lafayette), E. A. McIlhenny Collection, Avery Island, La.

Postcard of lilies in Jungle Gardens, circa 1930.

APPENDIX
A PARTIAL BIBLIOGRAPHY OF THE WRITINGS OF E. A. MCILHENNY

"Albinism in Mockingbirds." *The Journal of Heredity* 31 (October 1940): 433-38.

The Alligator's Life History. Boston: Christopher Publishing House, 1935.

"Alligators Interfere with Duck-Banding." *Bird-Banding* 8 (January 1937): 34-35.

"An Appeal to the American People." *The American Field* (30 March 1912): n.p.

"Are Starlings a Menace to the Food Supply of Our Native Birds?" *The Auk* 53 (July 1936): 338-39.

"At Home Fall and Winter." *The Illustrated Outdoor World* (May 1912): 13-17.

"At Home Spring and Summer." *The Illustrated Outdoor World* (April 1912): 26-30.

The Autobiography of an Egret. New York: Hastings House, 1940.

"Bamboo Growing for the South." *The National Horticultural Magazine* 24 (January 1945): 1-6. [Excerpt reprinted in *Bamboo* 30 (December 2009): 12-14.]

"Bamboo: A Must for the South." *The National Horticultural Magazine* 24 (April 1945): 120-125. [Reprinted in *Bamboo* 23 (June 2002): 23-26.]

"Barn Swallows Breeding on the Gulf Coast." *The Auk* 50 (October 1933): 439.

"Barn Swallows Breeding on the Gulf Coast." *The Auk* 52 (April 1935): 188.

Befo' de War Spirituals. Boston: Christopher Publishing House, 1933.

"Bird Banding at Avery Island." *Game Breeder and Sportsman* 45 (December 1940): 206-207, 218.

Bird City. Boston: Christopher Publishing House, 1934.

"Birds and the Winter of 1939-40." *The Auk* 57 (July 1940): 401-10. [E. A. McIlhenny et al.]

"Black Vulture Following Aeroplane." *The Auk* 55 (July 1938): 521. [With Rosemary McIlhenny Osborn.]

"The Blue Goose in Its Winter Home." *The Auk* 49 (July 1932): 279-306.

"A Brief for the Y-Chromosome." *The Journal of Heredity* 25 (October 1934): 406-408.

"Color of Iris in the Boat-Tailed Grackle (*Cassidix mexicanus major*)." *The Auk* 51 (July 1934): 383-84.

"Correction in Wording of Account of Hybridism between Turkey Vulture and Black Vulture." *The Auk* 54 (October 1937): 574.

"The Creating of the Wild Life Refuges in Louisiana." *Louisiana Conservation Review* 1 (October 1930): 23-25.

"The Creating of the Wild Life Refuges in Louisiana." *Ninth Biennial Report of the Department of Conservation of the State of Louisiana, 1928-1928* (1930): 139.

"An Early Experiment in the Homing Ability of Wildfowl." *Bird-Banding* 11 (April 1940): 58-60.

"Effect of Excessive Cold on Birds in Southern Louisiana." *The Auk* 57 (July 1940): 408-10.

"Feeding Habits of the Black Vulture." *The Auk* 56 (October 1939): 472-74.

"Florida Crane a Resident of Mississippi." *The Auk* 55 (October 1938): 598-602.

"The Garfish of Louisiana." *The Fish Culturist* 16 (1936): 25-28.

"Golden Eagle (*Aquila chrysaetos canadensis*) in Louisiana." *The Auk* 50 (October 1933): 431-32.

"How I Made a Bird City." *Country Life in America* 22 (1 September 1912): 23-28.

"How to Improve Missouri Duck Shooting." *Wild Life* (July 1917): n.p.

"A Hybrid between Turkey Vulture and Black Vulture." *The Auk* 54 (July 1937): 384.

"Iris: What They Are and How to Grow Them in the South." *Southern Florist and Nurseryman* (20 October 1939): n.p.

"Life History of the Boat-Tailed Grackle in Louisiana." *The Auk* 54 (July 1937): 274-95.

"A List of the Species of Anseres, Paludicolae, And Limicolae Occurring in the State of Louisiana." *The Auk* 14 (July 1897): 285-89.

"Louisiana Gulf Coast Club and Game Conservation: A Story of the Club and Its Purposes." *The Sporting Goods Salesman* (November 1923): 11-13, 26, 28.

"The Louisiana Refuges." *Recreation* (March 1915): 144-45.

"Major Changes in the Bird Life of Southern Louisiana during Sixty Years." *The Auk* 60 (October 1943): 541-49.

"A New Sport: The Capture and Banding of Birds at Night." *American Forests* 46 (October 1940): 439-41, 464.

"Notes on Incubation and Growth of Alligators." *Copeia* (30 July 1934): 80-88.

"Notes on the Five-Lined Skink." *Copeia* (31 December 1937): 232-33.

"On the Distribution of *Quiscalus* in Louisiana." *The Auk* 53 (October 1936): 416-17.

"The Passing of the Ivory-Billed Woodpecker." *The Auk* 58 (October 1941): 582-84.

"Pure Bred Mallard Versus Puddle and Call Duck." *Bulletin of the American Game Protective Association* (1 February 1917): n.p.

"Purple Gallinules (*Ionornis martinica*) Are Predatory." *The Auk* 53 (July 1936): 327-28.

"A Reason for Wild Life Conservation in Louisiana." *Louisiana Conservation Review* 1 (June 1931): 15, 46-47.

"A Record of Birds Banded at Avery Island, Louisiana, during the Years 1937, 1938 and 1939." *Bird-Banding* 11 (July 1940): 105-109.

"Results of 1936 Bird Banding Operations at Avery Island, Louisiana, with Special References to Sex Ratios and Hybrids." *Bird-Banding* 8 (July 1937): 117-21.

"Results of 1940 Bird Banding at Avery Island, Louisiana, with Special Account of a New Banding Method." *Bird-Banding* 13 (January 1942): 19-28.

"Returns of Banded Ducks Liberated outside Their Migration Route." *Bird-Banding* 1 (October 1930): 189-90.

"Robins Nesting in Extreme Southern Louisiana." *The Auk* 50 (October 1933): 439-40.

"Sex Ratios in Wild Birds." *The Auk* 57 (January 1940): 85-93.

"Sex Ratios in Wild Birds." *Game Breeder and Sportsman* 46 (April 1941): 64-65, 76.

"Some Interesting Records from Birds Banded at Avery Island, Retaken during the Winter of 1940-1941." *Bird-Banding* 12 (October 1941): 168-73.

"Twenty-Two Years of Banding Migratory Wild Fowl at Avery Island, Louisiana." *The Auk* 51 (July 1934): 328-37.

"An Unusual Feeding Habit of the Black Vulture." *The Auk* 62 (January 1945): 136-37.

"Unusual Feeding Habits of Some of the Ardeidae." *The Auk* 53 (October 1936): 439-40.

"An Unusual Migration of Broad-Winged Hawks." *The Auk* 56 (April 1939): 182-83.

"Unusual Plumage of Domestic Mallard Ducks." *The Journal of Heredity* 32 (January 1941): 19-21.

"The Vermilion Flycatcher in Louisiana." *The Auk* 52 (April 1935): 187.

"Whooping Crane in Louisiana." *The Auk* 55 (October 1938): 670.

The Wild Turkey and Its Hunting. Garden City, N.Y.: Double Day, Page and Company, 1914. [Charles L. Jordan manuscript finished on original author's death by E. A. McIlhenny.]

"The Wild Turkey and Its Hunting." *The Illustrated Outdoor World* (December 1912): 5-9.

"Will Mexico Help?" *The Illustrated Outdoor World* (May 1912): n.p. [With Charles Willis Ward.]